Whatchu Know About Mosses, Homeboy?

Grind by Zeeshan Mahmud

"A rolling stone gathers no moss." Proverb

"Never complain. Never explain."
Kate Moss

Humble brag

Alright, listen the f*** up. You think you know nature? Nah, you don't know s*** until you know mosses. And I know everythang 'bout 'em. I bet I can tell more yarns about mosses than your momma's grandma.

Yo. You bet your a– this ain't gon be anothuh' un' of them' books. Well yeah homes. 👍

Let's get started. These little green m********s been running their game since before the dinosaurs even figured out how to walk straight. That's right—450 million years of straight-up hustling, no roots, no seeds, no fs given.

Mosses ain't out here flexing with flowers or flashy a** fruits. Nah, they keep it low-key, just vibes. They pull water straight out the air, like, "Who needs roots, b****?" And guess what? They can chill on rocks, trees, sidewalks, even your busted-ass roof, making the rest of the plant world look like amateurs.

You wanna talk survival? These green badasses can straight-up pause their whole life when s*** gets rough—dry as f*** one day, soaking up water like a sponge the next. They've been thriving in places where most plants wouldn't last five minutes: Arctic tundra, deserts, your crusty backyard.

But don't get it twisted. These mossy **aholes aren't just survivors—they're straight-up heroes. Cleaning the air? Check. Soaking up rainwater so your basement doesn't flood? Check. Cooling the planet? F*** yeah, check.

So crack open this book and learn about the OGs of the plant kingdom. Mosses don't play games, and after reading this s***, neither will you. Time to get schooled, homeboy. Let's f***ing go.

Let's get down and dirty

Alright, lemme drop some moss knowledge on y'all real quick. Mosses are the OG tiny-ass plants from the division Bryophyta—yeah, that's right, some real Latin s***. These little green homies don't need no flowers, no seeds, and sure as hell no vascular flex like those fancy-ass trees. Nah, mosses keep it simple: tiny leaves, one cell thick, chillin' on a baby stem that barely does s*** to move water around. They like, "Yo, water, just roll through my crib wherever you want."

You've probably seen moss rolling deep in damp, shady spots, forming thick-ass carpets like they own the joint. Most of them stay short—like 0.2 to 10 cm tall—but don't sleep on *Dawsonia*, the big boss of moss, towering at a whopping 50 cm. That's like Shaq in the moss world. And guess what? There's about 12,000 species out there doing their thing.

You think you know mosses? Hell nuh bruh—mosses ain't lichens, liverworts, or hornworts. Yeah, they might look like cousins, but nah, they ain't even related. And those so-called "reindeer moss" and "Iceland moss"? Total posers. They're lichens, which are fungus and algae shacked up together like a weird fungal Airbnb. Mosses are plants, period.

Here's the real wild s***: mosses run their life cycle backwards compared to most plants. They spend most of their time in the haploid gametophyte phase—yeah, science s***—which means they're rocking single chromosomes while vascular plants are out here all diploid and bougie.

But don't sleep on their hustle. Mosses are out here running the game in habitat restoration, soaking up water like a green sponge (up to 20 times their weight!), and holding down the peat industry

(*Sphagnum* gang, stand up). Back in the day, folks even used moss for insulation, like "F*** fiberglass, gimme that moss drip."

So next time you see some moss, don't just walk by like a fool. Show some respect to these tiny, ancient, green m***********s holding it down since before your great-great-great-grandpappy was even a thought.

Scientific Classification of Mosses

- **Kingdom**: Plantae
- **Division**: Bryophyta
- **Class**: Bryopsida (most mosses belong here, but there are others)
- **Order**: Varies (e.g., Hypnales, Polytrichales)
- **Family**: Varies depending on the moss species
- **Genus & Species**: Thousands of species, like *Sphagnum*, *Polytrichum*, and *Funaria*.

Differences Between Mosses, Lichens, and Algae

1. Mosses (Bryophytes)

- **True Plants**: Mosses are part of the plant kingdom and have a simple structure but still photosynthesize.
- **No Vascular Tissue**: They lack xylem and phloem, so they absorb water directly through their leaves.
- **Reproduction**: Mosses use spores, not seeds. They also need water for sperm to swim to the egg.
- **Structure**: Made of tiny leafy shoots and rhizoids (not true roots).
- **Environment**: Thrive in damp, shady places but can survive harsh conditions.

2. Lichens

- **Not Plants**: Lichens are a *symbiotic partnership* between a fungus (provides structure) and algae or cyanobacteria (provides food through photosynthesis).
- **Independent Classification**: Lichens aren't classified as plants or fungi; they're an ecological combo deal.

- **Environment**: Super tough—lichens can grow on rocks, in deserts, or in Arctic tundra.
- **Reproduction**: They don't produce spores like mosses but propagate through fragments containing both fungal and algal components.

3. Algae

- **Diverse Group**: Algae aren't plants but belong to various groups like protists (*Chlamydomonas*) or even cyanobacteria (which are technically bacteria).
- **Aquatic**: Most live in water, though some are terrestrial.
- **Structure**: Lack true roots, stems, or leaves, and their forms can range from single-celled organisms to large seaweeds.
- **Photosynthesis**: Like mosses and lichens, algae photosynthesize, but they don't rely on other organisms (as in lichens).

Key Differences

Feature	Mosses	Lichens	Algae
Kingdom	Plantae	Fungi + Algae/Cyanobacteria	Protists, Plantae, or Cyanobacteria
Structure	Leafy shoots, rhizoids	Fungal + algal combo	Varied, no true leaves/roots
Habitat	Damp/shady	Almost anywhere	Mostly aquatic
Reproduction	Spores	Fragments	Varied (spores, division)

In short:

- **Mosses** = tiny, badass plants.
- **Lichens** = fungi renting an algae roommate.
- **Algae** = water-loving photosynthesizers, single or multicellular.

Psssshhh…. You know nothin' homes

Yo, we back in the moss dojo, droppin' that Bryophyta heat. Mosses are them small, non-vascular, herbaceous hustlers, out here soaking up water and nutrients straight through their leaves like, "Roots? F*** that, we got this!" They be sipping sunlight and carbon dioxide to whip up food through photosynthesis like green chemists in the hood.

Now here's the kicker: mosses don't play the fungi game like vascular plants with their mycorrhizal hookups. Nah, mosses roll solo. But hold up—they still got some shady fungi (bryophilous ones) kicking it in their pads. These fungi can be mutualists, parasites, or just freeloading saprotrophs, but mosses don't sweat it; they've seen worse.

Moss Anatomy: Built Different

- **Leaves**: Single-layered, no air pockets, rocking a midrib (a.k.a. the "nerve"). Sometimes the leaf tips even flex a white hair point like they're flossing on liverworts.
- **Stems**: They can grow straight up (acrocarp) or spread out like a lazy boy (pleurocarp).
- **Rhizoids**: Think of these like the bootleg version of roots—threadlike anchors holding moss down without absorbing any nutrients.

Spore Life is the Good Life

Mosses keep it spore-real. No seeds, no flowers, just spore capsules chillin' on long stalks. When it's time to level up, the sporophyte generation pops in—doing a little photosynthesis but still mooching water and nutrients off the gametophyte like that broke friend who never pays rent.

- **Sporangia Game**: Moss spore capsules are like single-child families—one per stalk. Liverworts? Nah, they're out here with multiple sporangia like they're flexing a bigger crew.

How Mosses Check Liverworts

Liverworts be lookin' like mosses' lame cousins, but here's the tea:

- Mosses got **multi-cellular rhizoids**, while liverworts out here with single-cell rhizoids.
- Moss leaves ain't no three-rank arrangement mess; they're straight-up wild, free, and ready to photosynthesize.
- Spore capsules in mosses take their sweet time maturing after the stalk grows, while liverworts rush the whole thing—amateurs.

The Stomata Saga

Now, here's some moss trivia for the nerds: in the OG moss classes like *Takakiopsida* or *Sphagnopsida*, stomata are either non-existent or fake as hell (pseudostomata). But the newer moss cliques? Stomata's been lost and found like 60 damn times. Evolution's got jokes.

Why Moss is the MVP

Moss is out here running sh**:

- Restoring habitats like a damn eco-hero.
- Soaking up water like a sponge on steroids.

- Flexing in peat bogs (*Sphagnum* gang forever).

So next time you're out there, kneel down and peep that moss up close. It's out here surviving, thriving, and flexin' while the rest of the plant world stays thirsty. Respect the moss grind, homie.

Mosses are gangsta AF

Mosses, the unsung champions of survival, have a life cycle that's nothing short of wild. These little green dynamos operate in two modes: haploid and diploid, flipping the genetic switch only during their sporophyte stage. Things kick off with a spore sprouting into a protonema—a lush, green carpet that's the OG foundation for moss growth. This protonema then gives rise to gametophores, where the party really starts.

Picture this: male and female organs, antheridia and archegonia, chilling on gametophyte stems. Mosses, ever the romantics, need water for their sperm to literally swim their way to the egg—talk about commitment. Some even amp it up with "splash cups," launching sperm across decimeters like tiny botanical cannonballs.

Post-fertilization, a sporophyte bursts forth, rocking a long seta and a spore-packed capsule topped by a calyptra. Once matured, spores rain down to keep the cycle alive. Some mosses, like *Sphagnum*, turn this into an aerial spectacle, launching spores with G-force rivaling fighter jets.

And it's not just wind doing the heavy lifting—mosses have side hustles. Microarthropods, wooed by pheromones, act as moss matchmakers, boosting fertilization rates. For the drama queens like *Splachnum sphaericum*, there's insect-attracting stink tactics, luring flies to spread spores via dung.

When life's tough? Mosses don't sweat it. They go asexual, cloning themselves with nifty structures like gemmae. Resilience, thy name is moss.

Dwarf Males

Mosses don't shy away from innovation, especially when it comes to dwarf males. These tiny males, often mere millimeters in size, emerge from spores that land on female shoots. In some species, their petite stature is hardwired genetically, with every male destined to stay small. More often, it's environmental; males that land on females stay dwarfed, while those landing elsewhere can grow to rival females in size. Transplanting these dwarf males away from their host females allows them to sprout into larger forms, hinting at a female-secreted substance—perhaps auxin—that curtails their growth and hastens sexual maturity.

Why the shrinkage? Proximity. Dwarf males sidle up close to female reproductive organs, boosting fertilization efficiency. The relationship is clear: more dwarf males, higher fertilization rates. These pint-sized partners are no fluke—they pop up across unrelated moss lineages and may be more common than once thought, especially among dioicous pleurocarps, where an estimated 25-50% feature dwarf males.

Whachu know 'bout DNA Repair homes?

Mosses like *Physcomitrium patens* take DNA repair as seriously as a ticking time bomb. This moss has become a poster child for studying homologous recombination, the plant world's go-to mechanism for patching up double-strand DNA breaks. When repair fails, the fallout ranges from cell dysfunction to infertility during meiosis. Thanks to its sequenced genome, researchers have pinpointed several repair genes in *P. patens*, shining a light on how plants deal with genomic damage.

Take the RpRAD51 gene: it codes for a protein pivotal to homologous recombination. Mutant mosses missing functional RpRAD51 struggle with double-strand break repairs. Likewise, mutants lacking key MRN complex proteins (Ppmre11 and Pprad50) exhibit impaired DNA repair, stunted growth, and developmental hiccups. In mosses, as in life, resilience is all about fixing what's broken.

How them classified tho?

Yo, moss ain't just some punk-ass greenery chillin' in shady corners—it's got a whole damn *division* to its name. We talkin' Bryophyta, aka the OG crew of nonvascular plants, hangin' with their homies, liverworts, and hornworts. They even rolled up in a clique called Setaphyta. Think of them as the Nature Mafia, low-key ruling moist spots and ancient lands like they own it.

Now, inside this Bryophyta fam, you got 8 exclusive classes, like Takakiopsida (the cryptic ones) and Polytrichopsida (the beefy, heavyweight champs). But let's not front—Bryopsida's the boss here, reppin' 95% of the species. That's like controlling the whole damn plant underworld.

Sphagnopsida? They're the peat-moss gang, the eco-CEOs of acidic bogs. They got these big-ass dead cells that store water like nature's sponges. Also, their sporangia? That sh*t explodes like it's straight outta a sci-fi flick.

Andreaeopsida and Andreaeobryopsida? Fancy af, splitting sporangium like some bougie drama queens. Then there's Polytrichopsida, flexing parallel lamellae—basically the Lamborghini fins of the moss world. And let's not forget Dawsonia superba, the skyscraper of mosses, hittin' 40cm like a green giant.

Fossil Records?

Mosses been out here since the Permian, maybe even the Carboniferous, laying low 'cause their soft-ass bodies don't fossilize well. But here's the kicker: 470 million years ago, these little bastards started playing atmospheric Jenga, sucking up CO2, and kicking off the Ordovician ice ages. Yeah, mosses basically said, *"Climate change? Hold my spores."*

Ecology Hustle:

Mosses are like the ultimate squatters—they'll roll up anywhere: rocks, damp logs, shady soil, and even busted city sidewalks. They're not parasitic, though; moss plays fair, even when it's crashing at a tree's place. Some badass species like Fontinalis (water moss) dive deep, thriving underwater, while Sphagnum grows long af in bogs, turning entire swamps into spongy empires.

But moss got conditions, yo. Needs water to hook up (fertilization), but if it dries out? No worries—they'll resurrect like nothing happened. Also, if you're in the Northern Hemisphere, check that north side of trees and rocks. Moss likes it shady and moist, like it's too cool for the sunny side.

Nitrogen Fixer Extraordinaire

Mosses team up with cyanobacteria like a green version of Breaking Bad. These blue-green bacteria fix nitrogen, moss shares the loot with the whole forest, and everybody thrives. It's a win-win hustle, but only if the moss decides to get disturbed—like after a fire or drought—so it can spread the wealth.

How is your growth game yo?

Cultivation

Moss plays a multifaceted role in horticulture and landscaping, serving as both an intentional feature and an unintentional presence.

Moss Lawns

Moss lawns epitomize serenity and timelessness in garden design, particularly in Japanese aesthetics. In temple gardens, moss forms lush, calming carpets, blending harmoniously with natural landscapes. Cultivation involves transplanting moss from its natural habitat or allowing spores to colonize prepared surfaces like brick, wood, or porous concrete. Acidic preparations, such as mixtures of moss, water, and buttermilk, can accelerate growth.

In regions like the Pacific Northwest, moss lawns thrive naturally in cool, moist climates, eliminating the need for mowing or irrigation. Iconic examples include the moss garden at the Bloedel Reserve, created through ecological thinning and natural moss colonization.

Green Roofs and Walls

Moss is an ideal candidate for green roofs and walls due to its lightweight nature, high water absorption, and minimal maintenance. It thrives without fertilizers, tolerates drought, and requires shallow substrates, making it a sustainable alternative to traditional plants. Properly chosen species adapt seamlessly to local climates, requiring no irrigation after establishment.

Mosseries

In the late 19th century, moss-collecting sparked the creation of mosseries—structures designed to showcase and cultivate moss. These shaded, slatted wooden enclosures were moistened regularly to sustain growth, combining functionality with ornamental value.

Aquascaping

Aquatic mosses feature prominently in aquascaping, enhancing both aesthetic appeal and water chemistry in aquariums. Their slow growth, hardiness, and low nutrient requirements make them compatible with fish habitats and low-maintenance setups.

Growth Inhibition

Despite its virtues, moss can become invasive in nurseries, lawns, and other settings. Controlling moss involves altering environmental factors or applying chemical treatments. Effective methods include:

- Improving drainage and exposure to sunlight.
- Encouraging competitive plant growth by raising soil pH with lime.
- Mechanically disturbing moss beds.
- Applying ferrous sulfate or similar products, which target moss while benefiting grasses.

Preventing moss regrowth necessitates addressing the conditions that favor its proliferation, ensuring a balance between aesthetic use and practical management.

USES OF MOSS

Traditional Uses

Moss has been a badass natural resource for preindustrial societies worldwide:

- **Insulation and Bedding:** Circumpolar peoples, including Sámi and North American tribes, relied on moss for bedding, clothing insulation, and filling gaps in structures like log cabins and longhouses. Moss-packed boots of Ötzi the Iceman are a testament to this ingenuity.
- **Medical and Hygiene Applications:** Moss's insane fluid-absorbing capacity made it useful for diapers, menstrual pads, and wound dressings. Native Americans took this to the next level, using moss in salmon preparation and food storage.
- **Food Use:** Finland used peat moss in famine bread, and Neanderthals from El Sidrón apparently chowed down on moss alongside pine nuts and mushrooms—yes, moss on the menu!
- **Fire Extinguishing:** In rural UK, *Fontinalis antipyretica* moss was the ultimate fire extinguisher, thanks to its water-retaining powers.

Commercial Uses

Moss also brings its A-game to modern commerce:

- **Horticulture and Floristry:** Sphagnum moss, a water-absorption beast, is harvested for nurseries and used as a growing medium or soil additive.

- **Peat Fuel and Whisky:** Decaying Sphagnum is the major component of peat, essential in fueling fires and flavoring Scotch whisky.
- **Medical Applications in War:** In World War I, Sphagnum was the OG wound dressing, outperforming cotton with its superior liquid absorption, antibacterial properties, and comfort.
- **Decor:** In Mexico, moss lights up Christmas decorations, giving festivities a natural touch.

Biotechnology and Urban Innovation

Modern science isn't sleeping on moss either:

- **Biotech Rockstar:** *Physcomitrium patens* is a genetic goldmine, used for improving crops, producing complex biopharmaceuticals, and even studying human health.
- **City Trees:** London introduced moss-packed "City Trees" with air-cleaning superpowers equivalent to 275 trees, kicking nitrogen oxides to the curb and purifying urban air.

This tiny plant continues to show up in badass ways, from prehistoric survival to biotech and eco-innovation today.

Name'm then!

How many mosses can you name brotherman? Here's a list of 20 important moss species:

1. **Sphagnum moss** (*Sphagnum spp.*)
2. **Haircap moss** (*Polytrichum spp.*)
3. **Cushion moss** (*Leucobryum glaucum*)
4. **Spanish moss** (*Tillandsia usneoides*)
5. **Common fern moss** (*Thuidium delicatulum*)
6. **Rock moss** (*Grimmia spp.*)
7. **Broom moss** (*Dicranum spp.*)
8. **Tree moss** (*Usnea spp.*)
9. **Sheet moss** (*Hypnum spp.*)
10. **Ceratodon moss** (*Ceratodon purpureus*)
11. **Fork moss** (*Dicranum polysetum*)
12. **Pillow moss** (*Brachythecium spp.*)
13. **Marsh moss** (*Calliergonella cuspidata*)
14. **Feather moss** (*Pleurozium schreberi*)
15. **Pine moss** (*Leucobryum glaucum*)
16. **Fern moss** (*Hypnum cupressiforme*)
17. **Moss fern** (*Selaginella spp.*)
18. **Plaited moss** (*Antitrichia curtipendula*)
19. **Beard moss** (*Usnea barbata*)
20. **Peat moss** (*Sphagnum cristatum*)

Not to be confused with...

Club moss refers to a group of plants from the family *Lycopodiaceae*, which are not true mosses but are often called "mosses" due to their similar appearance. They are more closely related to ferns and are part of the group of plants known as *vascular plants*. Club mosses have small, scale-like leaves and produce cone-shaped structures called *strobili* that contain spores for reproduction.

Some common species of club moss include:

1. **Lycopodium clavatum** (Ground pine or Tree clubmoss)
2. **Lycopodium annotinum** (Common clubmoss)

These plants are often found in forested environments and thrive in shady, moist areas. Despite their name, they are not true mosses because they have vascular tissue, allowing them to transport water and nutrients more efficiently than non-vascular mosses.

I love mosses of all shapes and colors!

Mosses, they ain't just plants, man. They got history, they got culture. Here's how mosses are rocking it across the globe, with all kinds of flair and uses.

1. **Sphagnum Moss**
   This moss is like that OG homie. Found in bogs, it's been used to stuff diapers, dress wounds, and clean up salmon before they hit the grill. Straight up, it's been saving lives in the trenches since WWI. Also, it's that magic moss that turns into peat for your garden or fuels up the Scotch whiskey game. Real one right there.

2. **Club Moss (Lycopodium clavatum)**
   This one's a throwback. People used to think it was some tiny pine tree back in the day. Used as insulation for boots in cold countries like the Nordics, and even in ancient rituals. Folks didn't just wear it—they lived in it. You ain't gonna freeze with these bad boys packing your clothes.

3. **Irish Moss (Chondrus crispus)**
   Nah, not the kind you throw on the ground for decoration—this one's all about the food. Irish moss is a

sea moss used in soups, puddings, and even for that healthy Caribbean punch. Packed with nutrients, this moss has been helping the culture survive. Get your vitamins on the go, like real-time hustle.

4. **Reindeer Moss (Cladonia rangiferina)**
   You think Santa's crew just pulls up and does their thing? Nah, they munching on this stuff. In the Arctic, reindeer moss is what the reindeer eat to survive. Back in the day, people used it as emergency food, too. You can say it's the real fuel for the north, keeping folks and animals alive when times get tough.

5. **Bristle Moss (Hypnum)** This moss is chillin' in the forest, used for everything from wound care to giving off that zen vibe in gardens. In Japan, it's in the temples, adding peace and serenity. People collect it, use it in bonsai, and get their inner calm going like a meditation session with a soft touch.

6. **Fern Moss (Thuidium)** They use this moss for making paper, and that's straight up craftsmanship, right? It's also one of the softest mosses around, used in the Pacific Northwest for creating a natural carpet in gardens. You got nature's luxury right under your feet, all while it keeps the ecosystem cool and hydrated.

7. **Cushion Moss (Leucobryum glaucum)**
   If you ever seen a moss that looked like a fluffy pillow, this is it. Used in Japan's moss gardens for its soft, plush look. This moss turns a lush garden into a tranquil scene that makes you wanna kick back and relax. Real zen, no cap.

8. **Fountain Moss (Mnium hornum)**
   Man, this moss is straight up hydrating. They use it in Europe to purify water, keeping things fresh like a natural filter. This moss's ability to hold moisture for days makes it the perfect partner for your garden, or even to decorate in water-based setups. It's all about that long-lasting coolness.

9. **Sheet Moss (Hypnum curvifolium)**
   This moss ain't shy; it grows fast and thick, like the hustle

you need when you're chasing that big payday. It's been used in everything from making wreaths to setting up floral arrangements in Europe. It's a part of celebrations, keeping things looking lush and green.

10. **Spanish Moss (Tillandsia usneoides)**

Down South in the U.S., Spanish moss is what gives those old oak trees their swag. It's not even a real moss, but it gives that eerie, hanging vibe, making it a staple in Southern Gothic culture. You see it in old towns, hanging from trees like it's got secrets to tell.

You down for some moss, homes?

Mosses ain't just for decoration, fam. They've got some real uses in diet, medicine, and herbology. Here's the breakdown of how people have been vibing with mosses in those areas:

1. **Moss as Diet**
   Yeah, mosses have been used as food for centuries in some parts of the world. Take **Sphagnum moss**, for instance. People in Finland used it to make bread during famines. And in **northern tribes** of North America, mosses were part of the diet too—used to absorb and store moisture in food, like a natural fridge. Moss is also packed with nutrients like iodine, fiber, and vitamins, making it a survival snack when there ain't nothing else.

2. **Moss in Medicine**
   Mosses have had a place in the medicine cabinet for ages, and they ain't just some ancient old wives' tale. **Sphagnum moss** was used as a bandage in World War I because it absorbs liquid like a boss—way faster than cotton and, they say, cooler and softer too. It's also known for being antibacterial, which helps keep wounds clean. On top of that, moss has been used for things like **wound dressings,**

menstrual pads, and **diapers** (Native Americans were ahead of the game with this one). Some mosses also have properties that help with **diarrhea**, **stomach issues**, and **inflammation**.

3. **Herbology with Moss**

   In herbology, moss isn't just some background player. It's used to support healthy **skin**, **liver**, and **digestive systems**. A lot of people in **folk medicine** use moss in tonics to **detoxify** or treat **coughs** and **chest issues**. Mosses like **Irish moss** (aka **Chondrus crispus**) are packed with minerals and are used in **herbal remedies** to soothe the digestive tract, reduce inflammation, and support the immune system. In **Caribbean herbology**, Irish moss is often used to make tonics that boost **energy** and **libido**, giving it that "superfood" status.

4. **Moss and Antioxidants**

   Moss isn't just chillin', it's also got some serious antioxidant action. People use certain types like **Reindeer moss** to combat **free radicals** and **cell damage**. Some mosses have compounds that can help detox your system, boost your immune response, and even work as a **natural anti-aging remedy**. Like, you can find **moss-infused oils** in some natural skincare routines for keeping your face fresh and youthful.

So yeah, moss ain't just a pretty face in the forest—it's got some serious life-saving, health-boosting potential if you know how to use it right.

Ima go forensic

Mosses have actually been used in **forensic science** for some cool applications, fam. Here's how:

1. **Time of Death Estimates**
   Mosses can help forensic scientists estimate the **time of death** by analyzing how they grow on a body. For example, mosses and other plants can start growing on a corpse after death, and the type of moss and how fast it's growing can help give an idea of how long a body has been exposed. Forensic botanists have used this to determine the **post-mortem interval** (PMI), aka the time between death and when the body was found.

2. **Trace Evidence**
   Mosses can be part of the **trace evidence** left at a crime scene. If a criminal is involved in some shady business and comes into contact with mossy areas (like forests, parks, or gardens), those moss particles can end up on their clothes, shoes, or even their car. Forensic scientists can identify and compare these moss particles with mosses found at the scene, which can link the suspect to the crime scene.

3. **Forensic Botany**
   In **forensic botany**, mosses help create a picture of the environment where a crime might have taken place. By studying the types of mosses around a crime scene, forensic botanists can determine things like **location** (whether the crime happened in a forest, on a building's roof, or in a garden) and **climatic conditions** (such as humidity or temperature) at the time of the crime. This kind of info can help build a timeline and context for the investigation.

4. **Environmental Mapping**
   Mosses, being sensitive to their environment, are also used

in **environmental forensics**. They can help forensic scientists understand the conditions at the scene, including whether the body was moved, what type of **pollution** or **contaminants** might have been around, and even how quickly the environment might have been changing at the time.

So yeah, moss ain't just chilling in nature—it's out there helping **solve crimes** and kick ass in **forensic investigations**!

Controh yasself homes!

Moss can be a stubborn little thing, spreading where you don't want it and thriving in places where you'd rather have something else. Here's how to **control** and **stop its spread**:

How Moss Spreads

1. **Spore Dispersal**
   Mosses spread mainly through **spores**, like little airborne seeds. These spores are released from the capsules on top of the moss, and if they land on a surface that's moist, shady, and nutrient-poor, boom, moss starts to grow.
2. **Vegetative Propagation**
   Moss can also spread by **fragmentation**—pieces of moss can break off and grow in new spots. If you disturb the moss, those bits can take root and establish themselves elsewhere.

How to Control Moss (in Lawns, Gardens, and Other Areas)

1. **Increase Sunlight**
   Moss loves shady, low-light spots. To control moss, try to **trim trees** or bushes that block sunlight. Let more light in, and you'll stress out the moss, because it thrives in the dark.
2. **Improve Drainage**
   Moss loves moist, poorly-drained areas. To control its spread, **improve drainage** by aerating your lawn or adding

sand to your garden soil. This will reduce the moisture content, making it less hospitable for moss.

3. **Adjust pH Levels**
   Moss thrives in acidic environments. **Lime** your soil to raise the pH and make it more alkaline. This can help deter moss growth by creating conditions where moss doesn't do well.

4. **Use Moss Killers**
   There are commercial **moss-killing products** available, most of which contain **iron sulfate** or **ferrous sulfate**. These products are effective at killing moss, but they won't prevent it from coming back unless you fix the underlying conditions (like moisture and shade).

5. **Physical Removal**
   Sometimes, you just gotta **pull the moss out**. Scrape it off with a rake or hoe, but be aware that moss can be persistent. Repeat this process regularly if the conditions haven't changed.

6. **Overseed with Grass**
   If moss is taking over your lawn, **overseed with grass** to fill in bare spots. Healthy grass can outcompete moss for space and sunlight. Make sure to water and fertilize properly so the grass thrives and the moss gets crowded out.

7. **Increase Airflow**
   Moss thrives in **stagnant air**, so improve airflow around your garden or lawn. Open up the area by removing obstacles and avoid over-watering.

How to Stop Moss from Spreading

1. **Regular Maintenance**
   Moss loves low-maintenance lawns and gardens, so make sure to keep up with regular **mowing, weeding, and aerating**. A well-maintained lawn will be healthier and more competitive against moss.

2. **Mulch or Ground Cover**
   In areas where you want to avoid moss, you can lay down a layer of **mulch** or use other **ground covers** to shade out the moss and keep it from spreading.

3. **Proper Watering**
   Moss loves damp conditions, so avoid **over-watering** your garden or lawn. Let the soil dry out between waterings to prevent creating an environment that moss loves.

Moss may be low-key persistent, but with the right approach, you can definitely control its spread and keep it from taking over your garden or lawn.

Mosses in Antartica?!? ZOMG!

Yes, mosses can be found in Antarctica, despite the extreme cold and harsh conditions. In fact, several species of moss are among the **hardiest** plants on the planet. They are found primarily in the coastal regions where conditions are less extreme, and there is a short growing season with a bit more moisture.

Key Points:

1. **Species of Moss in Antarctica**
   Some species of moss, like **Schistidium antarctici**, **Polytrichum juniperinum**, and **Bryum argenteum**, are native to the continent. These mosses can survive in freezing temperatures and grow in **moist, sheltered spots** such as under rocks or in snowmelt pools.
2. **Adaptations**
   Antarctic mosses are adapted to survive in low temperatures, and they can withstand long periods of desiccation (dryness). They rely on **snowmelt** and **moisture** from the environment to sustain their growth during the short summer months.
3. **Limited Distribution**
   They are mostly found along the **Antarctic Peninsula**, which has milder conditions compared to the interior of the continent. Mosses can also grow on some of the **sub-Antarctic islands** where temperatures are slightly higher.

4. **Environmental Role**
   While not abundant, mosses play an important role in the
   ecosystem of Antarctica. They provide **habitat** for small
   invertebrates like springtails and mites and contribute to the
   nutrient cycle of these ecosystems.

So, while mosses in Antarctica aren't as widespread or diverse as
in warmer climates, they are definitely present and have adapted
to thrive in the harshest environments on Earth.

Moss economy yo

Mosses do have some roles in the **economy, trade, and industry**, although their usage isn't as widespread as other natural resources. Some specific uses include horticulture, medicine, bioreactors, and even environmental applications. The most notable moss in this regard is **Sphagnum moss**, due to its significant industrial applications.

Key Economic and Industrial Uses of Mosses:

1. Horticulture (Sphagnum Moss)

- **Countries Involved:**
    - **Canada, Russia, Finland, Estonia, Ireland, Latvia, Lithuania**
- **Use:** Sphagnum moss is harvested for use as a growing medium in nurseries. Its **water retention properties** make it ideal for soil conditioning and moisture retention in plants. It's also used in **floriculture** to line hanging baskets and containers.
- **Economic Impact:** The market for sphagnum moss, particularly in **North America** and **Europe**, is significant, with companies in countries like Canada exporting large quantities to **the US**, **Europe**, and **Asia** for horticultural purposes.

2. Peat Production (Sphagnum Moss)

- **Countries Involved:**
    - **Ireland, Canada, Russia, Finland**
- **Use:** The decaying moss in the genus **Sphagnum** is the primary ingredient in **peat**, which is harvested for various

uses, including as a **soil additive**, **fuel**, and even for **smoking malt** for Scotch whisky production.

- **Economic Impact:** The global peat market is **multi-billion-dollar**. In **Ireland**, peat is a traditional industry, though it has faced environmental criticism in recent years. **Russia** and **Canada** are among the largest producers, supplying peat globally for agricultural use.

3. Bioreactors (Moss in Biotechnology)

- **Countries Involved:**
    - **Germany, USA, Japan**
- **Use:** Certain species of moss like **Physcomitrella patens** are used in biotechnology for **genetic research** and **biopharmaceutical production**. This moss is used as a bioreactor to produce **complex proteins**, **enzymes**, and other valuable compounds.
- **Economic Impact:** The biotechnology sector, especially in **Germany** and **the US**, is heavily invested in moss-based bioreactors for industrial-scale production of **bioengineering products**.

4. Air Purification and Green Infrastructure (Moss Walls)

- **Countries Involved:**
    - **United Kingdom, Germany, USA**
- **Use:** Moss is used in **green infrastructure**, such as **moss walls** and **green roofs**, which help absorb pollutants from the air, reduce noise pollution, and promote energy efficiency in buildings. In cities like **London** and **Berlin**, these installations are marketed as eco-friendly alternatives to traditional urban design.
- **Economic Impact:** The market for **moss-based air purification** and **sustainable architecture** is growing, particularly in **Europe** and **North America** as cities adopt more green-building initiatives.

5. Pharmaceuticals and Medical Uses (Sphagnum Moss)

- **Countries Involved:**
    - **United States, Canada, Russia**
- **Use:** Historically, Sphagnum moss was used in **first-aid** during World War I for **wound dressings**, as it absorbed fluids rapidly and had **antibacterial properties**. It was also used for **diapers** and **menstrual pads** by Indigenous people in North America.
- **Economic Impact:** Though its use has declined due to synthetic alternatives, there's still niche interest in the medicinal properties of **Sphagnum** and its potential use in modern **biopharmaceuticals**.

6. Decoration and Crafts

- **Countries Involved:**
    - **Mexico, Japan, China, South Korea**
- **Use:** Moss, especially **reindeer moss** (Cladonia rangiferina), is used for decorative purposes during **festivals, holidays**, and in **crafts**. In places like **Mexico**, moss is used in **Christmas decorations**, and in **Japan**, moss is often used in **bonsai gardens**.
- **Economic Impact:** The craft market for moss is modest, but it's part of **cultural industries** in certain countries, where it's used for both decorative purposes and as part of traditional festivities.

Moss Trade and Export

- **Canada** and **Finland** are the largest exporters of moss for **horticultural** and **peat** uses.
- **Russia** and **Estonia** also contribute significantly to the **peat industry**.
- The moss industry is highly regulated in certain countries due to its **environmental** impact, particularly in the

collection of Sphagnum moss, which is slow to regenerate and sensitive to overharvesting.

Challenges and Sustainability

Mosses, particularly **Sphagnum**, are considered a **non-renewable** resource in certain contexts, and there are growing concerns about the **sustainability** of harvesting them. Overexploitation of **peatlands** can lead to **ecosystem degradation**, making it essential for industries to focus on **sustainable harvesting methods** and the **reforestation** of moss habitats. There's also increasing interest in **synthetic moss alternatives** and other methods to reduce the environmental impact of moss harvesting.

Conclusion

Mosses, while not a massive industry compared to other natural resources, still play an important role in sectors like **horticulture**, **biotechnology**, **construction**, and even **medicine**. The economic impact is especially notable in **Canada**, **Russia**, **Europe**, and **North America**, where moss products are integrated into various industries for both traditional and cutting-edge applications.